THE HANDBOOK FOR
CLOSET CONSERVATIVES

THE HANDBOOK FOR CLOSET CONSERVATIVES

How to Succeed in Today's Liberal World

LEFTEN WRIGHT

iUniverse, Inc.
Bloomington

The Handbook for Closet Conservatives
How to Succeed in Today's Liberal World

iUniverse books may be ordered through booksellers or by contacting:

iUniverse
1663 Liberty Drive
Bloomington, IN 47403
www.iuniverse.com
1-800-Authors (1-800-288-4677)

Because of the dynamic nature of the Internet, any web addresses or links contained in this book may have changed since publication and may no longer be valid. The views expressed in this work are solely those of the author and do not necessarily reflect the views of the publisher, and the publisher hereby disclaims any responsibility for them.

Any people depicted in stock imagery provided by Thinkstock are models, and such images are being used for illustrative purposes only.

Certain stock imagery © Thinkstock.

ISBN: 978-1-4759-7630-4 (sc)
ISBN: 978-1-4759-7628-1 (e)

Library of Congress Control Number: 2013902816

Printed in the United States of America

iUniverse rev. date: 3/8/2013

Why the Handbook for Closet Conservatives?

Elections may come and go. Democrats win. Republicans win. Independents threaten. It doesn't matter. The fact is the liberals have won.

Beginning with the presidency of Franklin Roosevelt, liberal causes—welfare, recycling, affirmative action, busing, gay marriage, Social Security, criminal rights, civil rights, climate change, the environment—have become the way of life for all of us, either by law or judicial decree. And if you have any doubts, you are wise to keep them to yourself, especially if you are in the media, the arts, academia, unions, or the government, or go to temple or live on the West Side of Manhattan, Scarsdale, Beverly Hills, or San Francisco.

If you are going to get anywhere, if you are going to be asked to top- or even middle-drawer dinner parties, to book clubs, or to join the PTA in Glencoe or San Rafael, your best bet is to go undercover. It is important that you know exactly what liberals really believe, what their real motives are, and how to pass as one of them.

Or you are toast.

A Note to President George Bush

I know you have a great sense of humor, so I'm sure you won't be miffed at my inventing the lines I attribute to you. I did it to make a point about liberals whose first line of defense is Bush-bashing whenever they screw up. You'll get the point even if they don't.

Leften Wright

The Climate Is Changing!
The Climate Is Changing!

Man, this global warming is cool! Conferences around the world in five-star hotels, gourmet meals, spa massages, and lavish parties where we bemoan the threat of a changing climate and form committees to discuss solutions. It's a threat (which the Republicans, of course, deny) that we must spare no tax dollar to combat. Whatever the cost, the price of *not* taking action is higher—sinking coastlines, drowning polar bears, etc.

Although so far—with all the regulations, warnings, and billions spent at international meetings year after year on finding ways to stop it—the climate continues to go its own way.

Which only means we have to spend more, meet harder. Last year we got together in Geneva—great crème brûlée—how about Vienna next?

Mmmmm … can't wait for that linzer torte.

If you don't want to arouse green suspicions, best not confront them head-on with the information that the climate has been changing for trillions of years. Sometimes it's cold, sometimes it's warm. People and other creatures have adapted. They've gone in for lighter clothes or heavier bear skins, and sometimes nothing at all—which has also affected the temperature. And that was well before the invention of the internal combustion engine.

Look, if you've made a career of fighting climate change, you don't want to hear that a lot of people might like the idea of being warmer. No more digging out of the driveway all winter. Lower heating bills. Extra months of tennis.

Today, in fact, in the northern regions of our planet, once frozen ground has thawed, turning into fertile soil that produces much-needed crops. And ice-blocked waterways have opened to navigation to the delight of the frozen people there.* There has been a stampede to Greenland by foreign governments seeking the minerals now accessible in the thawing earth.

Chicago has faced the problem by quietly preparing for global warming, rather than fighting it. Future building plans will build for a warmer climate. A *Boston Globe* article that has mysteriously disappeared from the files reports that many climate change experts believe that the best solution is to adapt rather than confiscate everybody's automobile. Wear lighter clothing, plant shade trees, and try tinted windows.

But that isn't what you say to people who are planning their next climate change meeting in Bermuda—or making a fortune from it, like Al Gore, who changed his economic bracket to the 1 percent by writing books and movies, speaking to the faithful, and being the celebrity sitting on the boards of companies like Apple. There's our answer. Do an Al Jazeera Gore.

Since we can't stop the liberals from pouring our tax dollars into stopping global warming, which is going to happen no matter what they do, let's profit from it. Check into companies that make climate change equipment, especially those on the Democrats' donors list. Find out what Nancy Pelosi is buying.

Is she big on Tommy Bahama?

Or some unknown OTC company digging in Greenland?

Go to it.

Might as well be a *rich* closet conservative.

---

* Elisabeth Rosenthal, "Race is On as Ice Melt Reveals Arctic Treasures," *New York Times*, September 18, 2012.

Same-Sex Marriage
No Issue

"Who was that lady I saw you dancing with last night?"

"That was no lady. That was my partner in his new chemise."

You may think *weird*, but if you want to be accepted in our liberal world, you say, "Gorgeous. I think I'll pick one up for my partner."

That just might put you on the fast track.

In case you're thinking that gay marriage is not what most people want, since most voters have rejected it, don't even bring it up. You will get looks. And fewer lunch invitations. In California a judge threw out the results of the vote. What gives them the right to do that? But in the 2012 election, several states voted *for* gay marriage as well as for Obama. Could it be that people are sick and tired of the issue, and they figure the only way to stop hearing about it is to vote for it already?

Or has someone been putting something in our drinking water?

It's Israel's Fault
If Only Israelis Weren't Jews, Their Success
Might Not Be So Hard to Accept

Anyone who reads the *New York Times* knows that Israel regularly kills innocent children because the Palestinian missile launchers are next to sandboxes. And Israel builds fences and makes Palestinians wait in long lines just to make it difficult for the occasional suicide bomber.

If you are going to pass as a liberal, you will have to restrain yourself when your friends denounce the only democracy in the Middle East—a democracy whose Muslim citizens actually have greater freedom than those in Muslim countries. It's part of the Jewish plot, of course, to undermine Muslim values.

And don't even mention the only water in the Middle East you can drink without fear.

And schools that teach *girls*.

And you certainly don't point out that the Jewish state has more PhDs per capita than any other nation in the world.*

Or that it is a center of technology.

And pharmaceuticals.

And exports some pretty cool shoes.

And looking at Jewish girls with PhDs in bikinis on Tel Aviv beaches is more fun than ogling burkas.

And then you add casually that those bikinis are made in Israel. And wouldn't it be nice if Hamas converted its missile factory into a shop making Fatah's Fashions? And started a trade war.

(What about Jihad Briefs? Shorts with a pouch for explosives in dynamite colors.)

---

* "The Economy of Israel," *Wikipedia*.

Demand That the UN Ban Offensive Humor

Two Palestinian women were sitting in a cafe, showing pictures of their children. "This is my oldest son, Fatah," one said proudly. "He became a martyr when he was eighteen." The other woman nodded approvingly. "And this is my daughter, Nadia. She's a martyr too." The mother beamed as she showed the last picture. "My son, Hasad. A martyr." The other woman thought for a moment and said, "They blow up so fast, don't they?"

"The only time I hear Rush Limbaugh is when a pickup truck stops next to me at a traffic light."
—Spoken by one laughing tennis player to another at the Boca Raton Tennis Club

You'd better not have acrophobia if you're going to pass as a liberal because you'll be doing a lot of looking down. Down at Republicans. Down at people who go to church. Down at people who read the *New York Post*. Down at viewers of Fox News. Down at red staters.

Liberals know that conservatives don't go to the opera, ballet or theater. They go bowling. They haven't a clue where to find the Metropolitan Museum of Art.

They watch television in their undershirts while guzzling a calorie-filled beverage from a can. If they look at a newspaper, they go straight to the sports section. Or the girls in bikinis with big boobs. They've never heard of NPR. They listen to Rush in their pickup trucks or in their underwear at the dinette table. They own guns.

The only time a liberal looks up to them is when they change their flat tire on the expressway, or risk their lives to rescue people trapped in the World Trade Center.

If you get caught listening to Rush, you quickly say you were trying to get NPR. Reception problems.

And if you want to relay some information you heard on Rush that those liberal dunderheads will hear nowhere else, you use the usual preface: "I don't know where I heard this but … they say Obama is gay."

Or, "Would you believe my plumber swears that Obama is a Muslim because he rushed millions to Egypt when the Muslim Brotherhood took over? And left our ambassador defenseless in Benghazi? I almost bashed him with his wrench except the toilet was backed up."

Ike, the Do-Nothing President

When the name Eisenhower comes up at the right (or is it *left?*) social gatherings, the proper liberal reaction is a kind of laugh followed by comments like, "He didn't do anything. He spent eight years on the golf course. Ha-ha."

Well, let's see now. He *did* end the Korean War, which Truman bumbled us into. And he *did* send the army to Little Rock, Arkansas, to escort the first Negro students into a segregated high school, which happened to be the most important government action in the civil rights movement. He said he did not approve of the government forcing integration, but it was the law and he would enforce it. Isn't that a novelty? He also started NASA, and after sending advisers to Vietnam who told us to stay out, he stayed out.

And Kennedy charged in, followed by Lyndon Johnson.

We know what they did.

If only they had done nothing too.

You might take a chance and suggest people read *The Best and the Brightest* by David Halberstam.* Since

---

* Halberstam claims that Kennedy went into Vietnam to prove that the Democrats were not soft on Communism.

he was a *New York Times* writer, you won't be suspected of heresy as your friends read about what those smart liberals did in Vietnam … and why they did it.*

And there's the national highway system, which liberals know Eisenhower built for General Motors.

All this happened after he was commander of the Allied Forces in Europe and led them to victory. But you don't bring these things up any more than you would admit to watching Bill O'Reilly.

I dated a girl in college who lived on an estate in Atherton with a pool, tennis court, stables, and a mother who was the Democratic National Committee woman for California. It was near the end of Truman's term, and in spite of being the laughingstock of the country, he intended to run again, much to the horror of party leaders like Anthea's mother.

At one of their Sunday brunches around the pool, she disclosed to me that the Democrats were planning to dump Truman and draft Eisenhower. Eisenhower, she panted, was the most liked man in the country and would breeze them to victory. She raised her third martini and beamed.

"Asshole," she said, straying from her Mills College English, when he announced to the press that he was a Republican.

---

* Milton Eisenhower, the president's younger brother, had served as director of several government agencies and was the president of three universities.

When Eisenhower was nominated for president, a reporter interviewing his mother said that she must be very proud of her son.

"I'm proud of both my sons," she replied.

And that actually made the papers.

You Gotta Hand It to Those Muslims

If you're going to pass as a liberal, the first thing you have to know about Muslims is that there are a few bad apples in every barrel. A little terrorism isn't going to turn you into a right-wing bigot who goes postal over the plan to build a mosque near Ground Zero. Or cheers the New York City Police Department for keeping watch on Muslim Americans.

Instead, you will appreciate the artistic contributions of centuries of caliphates as reported in the *New Yorker* and displayed in the expanded galleries of Islamic art at the Met. You will learn about their acceptance of Jewish scholars. And their engineering feats—they brought fresh water in conduits down from the mountains into their palaces in Seville, delighting the slave girls in the harem.

You will read "30 Mosques In 30 Days" in the *New York Times* (July 19, 2012) and learn how Muslims invite even nonbelievers to feast with them during Ramadan, a holiday that seems to occur every other week.

You will delight at the growth of Muslim studies at our universities where genuine imams explain the beauty of the Koran. You will understand why they kill anyone who desecrates it.

When I toured Annapolis not long after 9/11, I was surprised to learn that the United States Naval Academy admitted students from Muslim countries, not only sharing with Egyptians, Saudis, and Jordanians what I thought would be military secrets, but also making special provisions for them—places to worship, approved food, observance of their holidays.

Which is, of course, the liberal thing to do. God forbid we should lose our sense of decency and make them feel untrusted.

I e-mailed a number of senators who I thought might be concerned, but received only form letter responses thanking me for my interest. One of them was John McCain, whom I bumped into several weeks later at LaGuardia Airport. He had appeared on *Saturday Night Live* the night before and looked pretty hip in his jeans and bomber jacket. With a nod at his companion who I assumed was a bodyguard, I asked the senator if it was wise, considering 9/11, to have potential enemies in Annapolis, West Point, and the Air Force Academy.

I thought if anyone would be upset, he would. He had not only attended Annapolis, but also had spent years in a Vietcong prison.

Wrong.

Looking uncomfortable, he said it was an American tradition that began long before he went to Annapolis. But he said he would look into it and dashed for his plane that was not yet boarding.

Who Did It?
Bush Did It.

One thing that convulses liberals is Bush-bashing.

Oil spill? *Bush did it.* Hostess crumbles? *Bush did it. Hurricane Sandy hits Staten Island? Bush* ... You get the idea. Go ahead, chuckle along and they'll think you're one of them. Don't even try reason.

"Take a Coon Out to Lunch"
Suggested Slogan for National Brotherhood Week, 1965

One of our top agency writers came up with that slogan when a bunch of us Madison Avenue guys were sitting around a table tossing out ideas for National Brotherhood Week. Every year there was a contest among advertising agencies to come up with the winning slogan. (That was in "The Madmen" days when our secretaries brought in the coffee, and we watched them bend over.) No longer do white Republican advertising guys kid around like that—not with what it costs to send kids to college. (And now our female bosses hump us, and we all get our own cappuccino from the one-shot machine.)

And yet, those madmen in gray flannel suits from Darien and Westport—when they weren't chasing their secretaries and angling for the corner office—did more than any freedom marcher ever did to end racism. They cast African Americans in television commercials, making them a normal part of American life.

You might want to mention to your liberal pals that Procter & Gamble, the epitome of white corporate America, did far more for equality than Jesse Jackson or Al Sharpton ever did. P&G produced the first all-black commercial. Defying warnings that the racist South would never use Tide again, they ran a commercial all across America with a black family praising its detergent.

Well, it turned out to be the most watched commercial of all time. People had never seen nonstereotypical blacks in a commercial before. They were transfixed. Instead of going to the refrigerator or bathroom, they watched. Sales soared. North, East, West, Midwest, and *South*.

Suddenly, companies were pursuing every African American actor waiting on tables and carrying bags and caring for white children. Black situation comedies followed. Black talk show hosts. As black people became accepted on television, they became accepted in life, a welcome guest in our living rooms. We discovered they weren't much different from white people, maybe funnier. Which, I suspect, was the most important factor in creating the color-blind society we would have today if liberal politicians would stop crying "racism."

It's safe to reveal this to liberals who don't really hate corporate America as much as they say they do. They will be delighted with this act of social justice, which they will label a smart way to sell their product—and they will be even more delighted if you tell them their P&G stock is raising its dividend. It's one of the winners in their portfolio along with Philip Morris and Coca-Cola.

By the way, it was the company we all hate that did more for women than Gloria Steinem ever did.

Philip Morris started the Virginia Slims Tennis Tournament, which put women right up there with the guys. Just ask Chris Evert. When the tournaments came to an end, it was she who went right up to the microphone and thanked their sponsor, Philip Morris, for making women's tennis what it is today.

But don't bring this up in liberal circles or you'll arouse their suspicions. They *know* it was affirmative action. You might as well wear your Ronald Reagan button.

I never had any problems with Netanyahu—except pronouncing his name. (Did Michelle *have* to serve him pork?)

George

Fracking
It Could Make Us Energy Independent
We've Got to Stop It

Heard about *fracking*? It's the latest plot by our energy companies to make America energy self-sufficient.

Hydraulic fracturing (fracking, for short) is extracting gas and oil from shale rock with water pressure, bringing out oil and gas from land once thought burned out. We're talking billions and billions of barrels of oil. The result? We're on the verge of producing more oil than any of our buddies in the Middle East.

From the way things are going, we will be energy self-sufficient in a few years. We won't have to bow and apologize to those sheiks, emirs, and ayatollahs. States like North Dakota, Texas, and Pennsylvania are already raking it in with new jobs, new construction, and new money.

Liberals, of course, are outraged. Sierra Club lawyers are heading to the courts to stop the ravaging of the landscape that was pretty ugly in the first place. And they are sounding alarms about contaminating the water table. They dispatch scare squads of kids to get people to keep that gas and oil in the ground where it belongs.

The truth is they are pissed that after all the billions of dollars the government has spent on sun power, wind power, ethanol power, and hybrid power, private industry has come up with cheap energy we can count on for decades from those awful Republican hydrocarbons. In fact, the word is that by 2020 we will out-produce all those Middle East nabobs combined. We are on our way to becoming the biggest gas and oil producer in the world. We will be *exporting* the stuff.[*]

Just don't be too smug about it among your liberal friends who won't be happy until everything is powered by the wind and sun, and the earth is sealed shut. Go ahead, lament with them about the assault on the earth and the threat to the water supply. Liberals love to lament. Their favorite word is *but*. *But* think what it will do to the farmers. *But* what about the hikers, the cyclists, the poor, the fish? Go ahead, lament with them as you fill up the tank with two-dollars-a-gallon gas.

But just to be on the safe side, you might want to drink bottled water if they frack in *your* neighborhood.

---

[*] Muller and Daniels: "the Fracker's Guide to a Greener World," *Wall Street Journal*, November 11, 2012.

McCarthyism
What Is It?

Check the box you think is correct.

_____ A witch hunt started by Senator Joseph McCarthy that swept the United States after World War II, destroying the lives of many innocent people he falsely accused of being Communists for his political gain.

_____ A sweeping prosecution of suspected Communists in our government after World War II, triggered by Senator Joseph McCarthy. Many were found guilty of giving Russia highly classified information that helped them take over Eastern Europe.

At the peak of the Cold War in the late 1940s, a slovenly dressed senator from Wisconsin—whose shirttail was never quite tucked in and who exhaled a whiff of alcohol—stood up in the senate and waved some papers listing, he declared, the many Communists and Russian sympathizers working in the state department.

Liberals were outraged. Not at the fact that our country might be in danger, but at the crude behavior of Joe McCarthy. President Truman laughed it off. The media demanded that McCarthy name names and then, when he did, accused him of naming names.

The Witch Hunt, as the media labeled it, had begun.

The most respected men and women in the state department were summoned before inquisitors—well-connected, urbane, witty graduates of Ivy League schools who glibly quoted Marx and Engels over martinis. Alas, many really turned out to be witches in Brooks Brothers clothing. Instead of being burned at the stake, they were given farewell steak dinners when they were reluctantly dismissed from their high-security-clearance posts and transferred to less sensitive positions. You don't turn your back on your fraternity brothers.

Ann Coulter writes that the word *McCarthyism* was actually coined by the Russians and quickly embraced by our elite universities and highly regarded publications. This chain-smoking oaf even suggested that the secretary of state at the time, Dean Acheson, was in the pocket of the Russians because he stayed loyal to "my good friend, Alger Hiss" when he was carted off to prison after being found guilty of a trivial matter of espionage.

One does not turn one's back on fellow Ivy Leaguers.

But he went too far, McCarthy. Intoxicated by his success, by the attention from the media, his charges grew wilder as his drinking grew more frequent. It was his questioning the loyalty of the military that did it. The Army-McCarthy hearings ran for thirty-six days on television, followed by eighty-six million viewers—the media frenzy brought him down. This upstart who craved attention, who was said to have questionable relationships with male staff members, who was covered by more reporters than the president, and who had Robert Kennedy on his team—crumbled.

He was censured by the Senate. But it no longer mattered. The people of Eastern Europe had been delivered into the paradise of the Soviet Union, which had been informed of our most secret strategies and bargaining positions by the "innocents" named by McCarthy.

We had been negotiating with a marked deck.

And down came the Iron Curtain.

Remember Walter Winchell? He was a newspaper columnist whose weekly radio broadcasts were among the most listened to in America. He was important enough to have a Hollywood movie made about him: *Sweet Smell of Success* starring Burt Lancaster. Winchell's influence was enormous. In the years leading up to World War II, he warned us of the threat of Nazism. In a clipped, shrill voice, he told the American public of Nazi influence in America; he named names fearlessly.

If only he had stopped there.

When the war ended, he was as concerned about the menace of Communism as he had been about Nazism.

He saw Russia as a threat, Communist sympathizers as dangerous. He was the one media star who supported McCarthy. And he vanished. The man millions of Americans listened to every week could not get a job.

Maybe it's the liberals who are guilty of McCarthyism.

See how far you'll get today if you are suspected of being a conservative, and you aren't Clint Eastwood.

George Bush is reported to have said,

"Instead of killing Bin Laden I would've waterboarded him. He had to have *some* information we could use."

(Bush won't give up on that waterboarding, will he? He must think it's something you do in a wetsuit.)

Movies You Will Never See
The Liberal Message Is the Normal Message

A movie that shows business in a favorable light instead of showing it poisoning our drinking water, harassing women, gunning down strikers, releasing cancer-causing vapors, stealing property from the poor, or trying to squelch Erin Brockovich. Don't even suggest a film showing the growth of a business that creates hundreds of thousands of jobs and makes products that make our lives better.

A movie that shows America in a good light. We either slaughter Indians, keep African Americans out of our neighborhoods, or lead empty lives that we enliven by jumping on top of our friends' husbands, wives, and teenage daughters. We drink a lot, take pills, and neglect our children who make out in our obscene SUVs.

A movie about the kidnapping of American hostages that portrays the actual perpetrators as monsters and does not seek to justify their actions by blaming the United States.

A movie that depicts the Hollywood Ten as anything but the victims of McCarthyism. Isn't it possible that just one of those card-carrying Communists who loved Russia and hated the United States might have been injecting anti-American messages into his films?

A movie in which a confessed former Communist names the members of his Communist cell and is praised for helping his country rather than scorned for being a squealer?

"There hasn't been a pro-American movie in twenty-five years," said Australian producer Bruce Beresford in 2009 when his film, *Mao's Last Dancer,* was released in the United States. It told the true story of a Chinese ballet dancer who spent a year with the Houston Ballet Company, then refused to go back to China. Liberal critics hated it.* The dancer actually *liked* the United States. How could Houston, Texas, be a major center of the arts? A big contributor is the Bush family. Really?

Yes, the Bushes did it.

---

* Mike Hale, "New to America, Discovering Its Glitter," review of *Mao's Last Dancer, New York Times,* August 19, 2010.

Who Said:

"Mahatma Gandhi ... isn't he the man who ran a gas station in St. Louis?"**

Sarah Palin

Hillary Clinton

Joe Biden

Bill O'Reilly

George Bush

Michelle Obama

If you don't know who Mahatma Gandhi is, Google him. Then the remark will be even funnier, especially from our secretary of state.

**Answer: It's our own Hillary, known for her sense of humor, who also said, "I'm getting the white vote" and "they have a plantation mentality. You know what I mean (wink wink)." Not to mention: "Jew him down." This is not something you bring up with your liberal friends. It would be like accusing the Virgin Mary of playing around. You might say you've gotta hand it to the lady for having balls. (Hillary later apologized for the Gandhi gaffe after being told it was in bad taste by an aide whom she reportedly called a "f...... Hindu lover.")*

"A few years ago, this guy would have been carrying our bags," Bill Clinton said of his wife's primary opponent— you know, the black guy who had the chutzpa to snatch the black vote right out of the Clintons' hip pocket and purse.

---

* "Clinton Apologizes for Ghandi Remark," *New York Times*, January 7, 2004.

The "Who Said It?" Game
A New Fun Game to Play with Liberal Friends

Each player writes quotes on slips of paper and tosses them into a bowl or a shoebox—as long as it isn't a Naot shoebox from Israel. You can enter as many quotes as you like. Here are a few suggestions to get you started:

"If you knew what communism was, you would hope, you would pray on your knees that one day we would become communist."
—Jane Fonda

"Better Red than dead."
—Vanessa Redgrave

"If George Bush is elected I'll leave the country."
—Alec Baldwin (who got fat instead of a passport)

"But we have to pass the bill so that you can find out what's in it."
—Nancy Pelosi

"If you can't find the right words, steal 'em."
—Joe Biden (reputedly)

After Biden was discovered to have a history of plagiarism not in his resume, his career soared. It was no big deal to the liberals who now talk of his making a run for the presidency.

"I was brought up in a country that relished fear-based religion, corrupt government, and an entire white population living on stolen property that they murdered for and that is passed on from generation to generation."
—Sean Penn

"It's the Jew producers in Hollywood who are holding down the blacks."
—Spike Lee

"You don't mind getting mugged in a bad neighborhood. All they get is your wallet. But don't go anywhere near Wall Street. They rob you of your life savings and your future."
—Whoopi Goldberg

"God damn America!"
—Reverend Jeremiah Wright leading his congregation at a Sunday service. You'll find it on YouTube if it hasn't been removed.

The Liberal Guilt List Contest
Whoever Adds the Most Could Win a Photograph of a Hollywood Star Who Is into the Right Causes

They say that right-wingers are happier than liberals. Of course they are. They don't care about the rest of the world. As long as they're safe inside their segregated community, they don't give a farthing about the victims out there. But liberals care. They feel guilty about them. They love to feel guilty so much they find victims everywhere.

Liberals feel guilty about

- the blacks they enslaved (six hundred thousand white men died to free them, but that will never be good enough),

- the Native Americans they slaughtered (gambling casinos won't do it),

- the Japanese Americans they put in camps,

- the animals they turned into coats,

- the flies they swatted,

- the handicapped in wheelchairs who went bumping down stairs for lack of ramps,

- the women with fat legs they excluded from boardrooms,

- the retarded people who were not admitted into graduate school,

- the single mothers they accused of being immoral and failed to support, making them lie in the beds they made out in,

- the gays who were called perverts and mocked with flouncy imitations,

- _____ (add your own, and good luck).

This page not meant to be blank.

Bush did it.

Happy 102nd Birthday
Granny ... Now *Strip*.

Every terrorist who has attacked us has been a young Muslim male. The shoe bomber. The underwear bomber. The guy who left a car with a ticking bomb in Times Square. The terrorists who bombed the World Trade Center the first time. And flew into it the second time. So what do we do?

If we were bigoted Reagan-loving right-wingers, we would nab every dark-skinned young man who heads toward an airline gate and waterboard him on the spot. But we are in the hands of liberals who do not want to offend the enemy by suggesting they are the enemy. So we pretend not to know what we know, and we go after the elderly on crutches, and toddlers who may be concealing weapons in their romper suits. Just because all the terrorists have been Muslims does not mean that all Muslims are terrorists.

Liberals love to cry Oklahoma City, as if they really believe a single act of terror is the same as an organized terror group that may strike anywhere at any time.

Not even a certified liberal is allowed to deviate from the Correct Thinking. Look what happened to Juan Williams, the African American National Public Radio commentator who said in a moment of candor that seeing a group of Middle Eastern young men board a plane with him made him a touch nervous. He was immediately fired, stripped of his ACLU pin, his Greenpeace tee shirt, his NPR tote bag—and exiled to FOX.

The Good News:

All this intimate inspection is said to be boosting sales at lingerie stores, which I hear now offer some very sexy undergarments designed for women over seventy who once barely made it to Kohl's. They are reportedly flying off the shelves. As well as in the air. Now that's a stimulus plan that's working!

Let Them Drink Ethanol

Look, the Government Can't
Be Right All the Time

(It was Bush's fault anyhow)

We thought liberals were surely in trouble when the *New York Times* turned against ethanol.*

In 1970, when our Arab pals cut off our oil supply and drivers were coming to blows in gas station lines, the *New York Times* and everyone else was screaming for the government to get into the fuel business and make the oil companies give us ethanol. You could make it from corn. Renewable. Unlimited. Everyone would profit. No more gas shortages.*

Well, *New York Times*, the government did what you demanded. At a cost of billions of dollars, it created a Department of Energy, which then created an ethanol industry so that today 40 percent of our corn crop goes to produce ethanol. The result: grain shortages, rising prices throughout the economy. Farmers are going broke, the poor in poor countries are going hungry, and

---

* Editorial, "One Bad Energy Subsidy Expires," *New York Times*, January 6, 2012.

it turns out that mixing ethanol with gasoline isn't such a good idea after all.

The blend yields about 30 percent less energy than gas alone, so mileage drops. And it costs more to ship and handle than gasoline. In the thirty-five or so years since the Department of Energy was created, it has spent billions of dollars on wind farms, solar companies like Solyndra—and its major accomplishment is ethanol.

But hold on. This doesn't mean the country is going to give up on the crusade to power everything by anything but fossil fuels. If we did, that would mean that Ronald Reagan was right when he suggested we abolish the Department of Energy.

Which is not something you bring up in the liberal world.

Integration, Not Education
Good News!
Our children may rank twenty-fifth in education scores,* but we're first in diversity!

You should know the right priorities if you're going to pass as a liberal. For years, American kids beat out all the other kids in the world in academic achievement. Math. Physics. Geography. Languages. But liberals put an end to that. The United States ditched education for integration. Now, our kids rank far behind those in other countries, even kids in India and China.

---

* From a speech by Pascal D. Forgione, US Commissioner of Education Statistics, whose renomination was blocked by the Clinton administration. He was hired as superintendent of the Austin (Texas) Independent School District.

I'll tell you, classrooms today warm a liberal's heart. No longer are they filled with those boring white kids who all look alike—kids who value education, and kids with parents who help them with their homework and have conferences with their teachers. Now every classroom is a United Nations of children—to liberals the UN is still a good thing—all relating in joyful harmony as they discover a multitude of cultures.

Our children may not be learning as much as they once did, since many of the bright, white kids have been replaced by less-bright kids of the proper color. But you can't have everything. This isn't China, thank God, where they give every educational opportunity to the most promising children. But our kids are sharing and understanding, and they reach out to one another, even to the funny-looking kid with the pierced lips. And isn't that what a real education is all about?

Right-wingers just don't get it.

What you do is ask, carefully, why the children of our liberal politicians go to private schools. The same politicians who oppose charter schools.

That might make them a little nervous.

So What's to Remember
about Pearl Harbor?
We Dropped the Bomb on Hiroshima

I just heard a song on the radio about Hiroshima. It was sung by a Joan Baez kind of balladeer who could not beat her chest severely enough to express her anguish at what this country did to innocent Japanese. She sang about the deaths, the devastation, the children on their way to school, and the lifetime radioactivity treatments for those who survived. Hiroshima heads the list of American atrocities that liberals love to recite—Japanese internment camps, Pinochet, separate drinking fountains, the DAR and Marian Anderson. (If you don't know who she is, get thee to Google immediately.) We are the criminals.

Funny, the Japanese don't seem to feel that way.

In Hiroshima, now a modern and prosperous city, there is a museum devoted to the atom bombing that put it on the tourist map. People from all over the world shuffle quietly past exhibits of heartbreaking photographs of scarred children, corpses, and rubble. Among them are leaflets dropped by the Americans, warning people to leave to escape the coming disaster. And there are warnings by the Japanese government that anyone caught picking up a leaflet will be shot.

There is a book in which visitors write comments. A movie on a loop runs nonstop, showing the devastation, the disfigured survivors, and the hospital run by Americans to treat survivors for the rest of their lives. There were a surprisingly fair number of survivors, since the rays of the bomb reached only so far. They radiated out as a circle from the point where it hit, and abruptly stopped, sparing all beyond the circumference.

Emperor Hirohito appears in the film. When asked to comment, he says, "It is all very sad—but, if you remember, there was a war on at the time."

Visitors are asked by a man with a video camera to give their reactions. Don't breathe a word of this to a soul, but I said, "It's too bad we couldn't have done it sooner."

The bomb brought an end to the war almost immediately, saving countless Japanese and American lives. It resulted in General Douglas MacArthur running Japan. One of the things he did was introduce flu inoculations, which were estimated to have saved more lives in a year than were lost at Hiroshima. Liberals, of course, know that his goal was to enrich the pharmaceutical companies.

The guide on our tour bus said that the bombing gave the Japanese a chance to rebuild Hiroshima into a modern, beautiful city where tourism flourishes. He said proudly that the city is a big attraction. Our ancestors must be very pleased.

Believe Me, Dan Quayle, You Are No Joe Biden*

When Dan Quayle misspelled potato as "potatoe," it made history. It was in newspapers, magazines (which were important then), television talk shows, even Broadway shows. It kept late-night comedians going for weeks. It was yet another gaffe by another dumb Republican—this time by George H. W. Bush's vice president. That "e" is in the history books along with the Gulf War and Nancy Reagan's china.

Well, let me tell you—Quayle doesn't even come close to smiling Vice President Joe Biden in the gaffe department. The problem is that the media doesn't give Biden the credit he deserves because he's a you-know-what-crat. Check out these Bidenisms, which make Quayle's goofs pale in comparison:

"You got the first mainstream African American who is articulate and bright and clean and a nice looking guy. I mean that's a storybook, man." (Biden referring to Barack Obama at the beginning of the 2008 primary campaign, January 31, 2007)

"John's last-minute economic plan does nothing to tackle the number-one job facing the middle class, and it happens to be, as Barack says, a three-letter word: jobs. J-O-B-S, jobs." (Joe Biden in Athens, Ohio, on October 15, 2008)

"Jill and I had the great honor of standing on that stage, looking across at one of the great justices, Justice Stewart." (Biden on January 20, 2009, mistakenly referring to Justice John Paul Stevens, who swore him in as vice president)

"His mom lived in Long Island for ten years or so, God rest her soul. And— although she's—wait, your mom's still—your mom's still alive. Your dad passed. God bless her soul." (Biden on March 17, 2010, speaking about the mother of Irish Prime Minister Brian Cowen who was very much alive)

"When the stock market crashed, Franklin D. Roosevelt got on the television and didn't just talk about the, you know, princes of greed. He said, 'Look, here's what happened.'" (In this interview with Katie Couric on September 22, 2008, Biden was apparently unaware that television did not exist in Roosevelt's time. FDR was known for his radio fireside chats)

"This is a big fucking deal!" (Biden caught on an open microphone congratulating President Obama during the health care signing ceremony, March 23, 2010)

"You cannot go to a 7-Eleven or a Dunkin' Donuts unless you have a slight Indian accent ... I'm not joking." (Biden to an Indian American man on C-SPAN in June 2006)

"Stand up, Chuck, let 'em see ya." (Biden to Missouri State Senator Chuck Graham, who is in a wheelchair, in Columbia, Missouri, on September 12, 2008)

If the president can say he's visited fifty-seven states when campaigning in Oregon in 2009, and thank the good people of Saint Paul when he is in Minneapolis, and it doesn't make the papers, then who is going to pounce on Joe Biden?

*From the vice-presidential television debate between Dan Quayle and Lloyd Bentsen who said, when the name of John Kennedy came up: "I knew John Kennedy and, believe me, Senator, you are no John Kennedy." Mr. Quayle was stunned and had that "deer in the headlights look" the New York Times reported in their own fair way. It was not until the next day that Quayle responded with, "I'm certainly not John Kennedy. I'm faithful to my wife."

Disguises to Wear While Shopping at Walmart

As a certified liberal, the only time to be seen at a Walmart is when you are carrying a placard and protesting. They have formed committees to prevent Walmart from opening anywhere there are people. The moment they are tweeted that Walmart is looking at property, they grab their signs and charge. The reasons are well known. Walmart, with its unconscionable, irresistible low prices drives out local mom-and-pop stores with their  lovable high prices. Not to mention the big W's well publicized low wages and sexism. But just between you and me, Walmart attracts the wrong kind of people for the liberal elite. You know what I mean—they aren't Nordstrom.

Loud, grabby minorities, the product of poor schooling and discrimination (*Bush did it*) pile into Walmart for its low prices, instead of supporting the gouging merchants in their own neighborhoods. They don't look good on liberal elite streets.

Our Weapon: The *Walmart Effect*

At a protest the other day, I noticed that three screamers had mysteriously disappeared. I looked inside the Walmart store and spied three suspicious-looking shoppers. One was in the men's underwear section, another at women's jeans, and the third at cosmetics. All buying. Not even a die-hard liberal can resist those price rollbacks. But you tell your liberal neighbors and golf partners that you shop only at unionized stores. That's what they tell *you*.

There are surveys that claim a Walmart store often brings more stores to an area than it drives out, actually creating more employment. A Walmart store becomes a shopping hub. The next time you're in a Walmart parking lot, notice the BMWs, Subarus, and Lexus vehicles. Take pictures of the license plates. You might want to use them someday.

The Poll Tax Is Back
(Voter Identification, My Ass)

All of a sudden a bunch of states are passing laws that require voters to show photo identification when they show up to vote. They claim they are trying to stop cheating. True, Florida just purged a few thousand names from its voting rolls because they happened to be dead, but liberals know who's behind it and what it's really about.

It's us racist conservatives trying to keep African Americans from voting.

Who are the people least likely to have a photo ID? You've got it—poor African Americans. We say *why shouldn't they be expected to have one just like everyone else*? They drive. They have passports. They have bank accounts, computers, and cell phones. They have credit cards. Some even pay taxes, or are smart enough not to. For some inexplicable reason, liberals look upon them as dummies the instant they enter a polling place.

Did you see *The Iron Lady*, the movie about Margaret Thatcher? Meryl Streep, playing Thatcher, asks, "Why shouldn't the poor pay taxes like everyone else for the benefits of living in England?" Would you believe it—

conservatives actually expect the disadvantaged to be as responsible as the rest of society. Surely President Obama, a whiz at bypassing Congress, can issue a decree to prevent this new form of poll tax. His friends at the Association of Community Organizations for Reform Now (ACORN) can help—the ones who aren't in jail.

As Joe Biden might say—*that's a hell of a lot of phony votes to piss away.*

Let Them Eat Only What We Say Is Good for Them
Mandatory Weigh-Ins to Begin

Regular weigh-ins of the American population will start next month. You will be notified where your scale center is located. They will be run by Michelle Obama squads who will set the weight guidelines for your age and build, and you will be taxed for every ounce you exceed that. The rich, of course, will be taxed at higher rates. Unfortunately, it's the poor who tend to be obese, since the rich eat healthier foods and have personal trainers. Maybe there should be a tax on personal trainers. (Is it possible the rich are smarter about diet *and* about making money? We'll have to level that difference.)

There will be no more advertising for soda, ice cream, cakes, or cookies. True, jobs might be lost at Coca-Cola and Entenmann's, but we'll have government programs for those people.

Also, everyone will be required to follow an exercise regimen until they have muscles like Michelle's. No exceptions, except for the very handicapped and union officers who may buy exemptions as they did with Obamacare. We may also exempt big contributors.

Al Gore will not be permitted to appear in public at his present poundage. Michael Moore will have to shape up. We will have a Guantánamo-type facility for the unbelievably fat. Since Obama is said to be a smoker, and smoking contributes to slimness, we may reconsider our policy toward cigarettes. Studies have found that thin smokers live longer than fat nonsmokers.

Those new cameras you see in supermarkets and restaurants are sensors to detect high-calorie foods. The average calorie count allowed in your shopping basket will be posted at the entrance and exit. If an electronic burp goes off while you are wheeling out your groceries, you will be wrestled to the floor. Some people might find these measures a bit dictatorial, but you will soon learn to appreciate them if you know what's good for you.

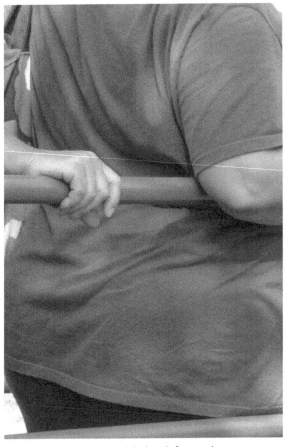

Dimensions will be established for airline passengers. Those who exceed the limits will be checked through with oversized baggage.

Let's Hear It for Zagat and Consumer Reports
They Dare to Praise Chick-fil-A

Yes, *that* Chick-fil-A! The anti-gay Chick-fil-A! The fast-food giant whose owner has publicly taken a stand against gay marriage. He speaks out against it at his church. He contributes to organizations fighting it.

Would you believe that *Zagat*, the ultimate guide for gourmets, not only rates fast-food restaurants, but also ranks Chick-fil-A best for quality of food, nutrition, service, ambience, and cost. And to make matters worse for the liberals, *Consumer Reports* has given Chick-fil-A its top rating, too.

I hear there have been threats. Something about a mob of very upset gay-rights people planning to storm *Consumer Reports* offices with same-sex kiss-ins and outings of some of their most important reporters. Liberal politicians in bed with gay-rights groups have announced that new Chick-fil-A's are not welcome in cities of such high moral standards as Boston and Chicago.

While protesters have organized some pretty heavy grope-ins at Chick-fil-As across the country, even more people, saying something about free speech, have swarmed in to buy all the damn chicken they can stuff in their mouths, raising sales to new heights.

Liberals are demanding that *Zagat* and *Consumer Reports* add a new category to their restaurant ratings along with cost, service and ambience—*political position*. So diners know exactly where a restaurant stands before they sit.

Come to think of it, that may not be a bad idea. We could go bipartisan with that one.

Bush is a dumb cluck!

"You Mother F***ing Jew Bastard!"
What do you do if you are Jewish and the liberal leaders you adore say things that sound suspiciously anti-Semitic?
You vote for them.

(Deep down you tell yourself they're really on your side.)

This was screamed by Hillary Clinton, it is said, to Bill's campaign manager, after he lost the race for reelection as governor of Arkansas. This is one of many colorful, ethnic expressions—such as "Jew him/her down"—that Hillary is said to use regularly. Her epithets have not diminished her appeal to Jews, nor did her kissing Yasser Arafat's wife, who had given a speech accusing the Israelis of poisoning Palestinian children. You gotta admire the gal's *chutzpah*. (A little joke here— chutzpah, for those in the red states, is a Yiddish word meaning "guts." It's very popular among liberals. You'd better know it if you're going to pass as one.)

All Obama has to do is suggest that Israel withdraw to its 1948 borders and his admirers find new reasons why he was right, was misquoted, or did not mean it the way it sounded.

And then there's Eleanor Roosevelt. Not once during Hitler's increasing persecution of the Jews did she express disapproval, let alone suggest that America might welcome refugees. When she finally expressed sympathy for their plight, it was with reservations. She wrote, "the Jewish people may be in part responsible for the present situation." She had something there. They were alive, taking up German space, and breathing German air.

She was, however, instrumental in rescuing refugee dogs. (Can dogs be Jewish?)

And, of course, it was the Republicans who had lost forty-eight out of fifty states to Roosevelt, who *forced* FDR to turn refugee ships back to Hamburg, where the passengers could get a direct connection to Auschwitz.

When it was leaked that Jesse Jackson, aspiring to be the Democratic presidential nominee, referred to New York as "Hymietown," Jews in Larchmont, New York held "Jews for Jesse" Coffees.

And don't think we're going to be fooled into going negative against Obama just because he has presided over the transformation of former Middle East allies into jihad states that hate us and don't like having Israel around either.

I once met Eleanor Roosevelt in a television studio where she was to appear in a pilot of a show in which she would have fascinating discussions with college students. The students waited eagerly to meet this legend who, when she arrived, headed directly to a girl wearing a sari, giving her all her attention. She barely acknowledged the Americans.

What Do You Do If You Pour Billions of Dollars into Housing for the Poor and You End Up with Mother Cabrinis Everywhere?
You Pour More

Every year we spend around $25 billion to build and maintain public housing and subsidize rentals.* It started with Franklin Roosevelt to bring the poor decent housing that, he said, the private sector had failed to do. They were only interested in building mansions for the 1 percent.

Since the liberals believed that people are shaped by their environments, they felt that if the poor lived well, they would gain self-respect, and they would study and work hard.

It did not work as planned.

The new tenants threw garbage everywhere, stopped up the plumbing, and ignored their kids who ran amok, forming gangs that preyed on other tenants. Pizza deliverymen and telephone repair guys traveled in pairs.

---

* Howard Husock, "Public Housing and Rental Subsidies," CATO Institute, June 2009.

As one project after another turned into a war zone and was torn down almost the day after it went up, the liberals insisted it had to do with the design, the architecture, and the location—not with policies that were turning people into irresponsible, dependent sloths.

It's a matter of education, said the compassionate liberals. We have to teach them the fundamentals of civilized living. It isn't their fault they are what they are after years of discrimination. People like George Bush did it. Their answer: build more public housing and spend more tax bucks.

Oppose public housing and you give yourself away as a heartless conservative. But here's a thought: require that politicians who promote public housing live in one of those projects with their families. Okay, maybe not for a year—a month will do it.

Also, require the people in the Department of Housing and Urban Development to try living in a project. Then they can *share*—that's today's word—the experience.

That may just inspire other ideas.

Here are some suggestions to improve public housing so that tenants don't feel like second-class citizens. How about rooftop pools? The roofs will have very high, strong fences, of course. Kids will be kids, and it would be best to avoid twentieth-story pushes. Indoor pools too—that goes without saying. You can't expect the 98 percent not to live like the 2 percent.

In New York there is a wonderful housing complex across from Lincoln Center whose performances the tenants rarely attend except to pick a pocket or two or case the parking garage for likely loot. The solution is simple: let's provide them with enrichment courses so they can appreciate the culture just outside their barred doors—and free tickets, of course, so they can experience it without working for it. I'm sure there is no end to amenities that will make people grateful for their subsidized housing and make them treasure it rather than trash it.

These are the kinds of suggestions that will allay any suspicions that you might be a heretic in the liberal world. The only risk is that they will carry them out.

When a Company Gets Too Successful
Sue!

Deep inside a government building in Washington, DC, behind an unmarked door, is a hidden department whose purpose is to keep an eye on American businesses and do everything possible to stop any that are growing.

Government people do not like those who make it on their own, especially when they live well, get quoted on the web, are admired for their success, and contribute to the Republican Party. Here is a partial list of companies the government has sued for one reason or another when they threatened to become too big for the bureaus:

Google
Apple
Microsoft
IBM
Staples
Boeing
Old Dominion Freight Line
HarperCollins, MacMillan, Penguin, Simon & Schuster
BAE Systems
Skechers Shoes

The government went after Google for conspiracy to restrain trade, even though the trade would not have been there had Google not started it in the first place. Staples got hit for trying to merge with Office Depot and create a monopoly. The government did not seem to know that to create a monopoly, Staples would also have to merge with CVS, Walgreens, Walmart, Kmart, and supermarkets around the country where millions of people buy their three-subject notebooks, ballpoint pens, and filler paper. Not to mention printer cartridges and disks. They hit on Boeing for building a plant in Alabama rather than in Seattle, where the union wanted it to be. Old Dominion Freight Lines, a trucking company, was stopped from firing a driver with a history of alcohol abuse—a violation of the Americans with Disabilities Act. IBM fought off the government for years.

I tell you, there isn't anything businesses won't try to get away with if not kept in the liberal crosshairs.

And if we don't keep on top of them, small businesses could grow into big, evil companies. It's happened.

Don't blame me for the Arab Spring.
I was in Crawford until summer.

GWB

He Was One of the Most Liberal Presidents We Ever Had, Yet Liberals Love to Hate Him
It Makes Them Feel Good All Over

Richard Nixon, the uneasy man in the black suit with shifty eye—from whom you would not buy a used car—did the following while he was president:

- ended the war in Vietnam

- established the EPA—yes, *that* EPA (Environmental Protection Agency)—cleaning up the air and water began in earnest with Tricky Dick

- increased the minimum wage

- increased Social Security benefits

- froze wages, prices, and rents in an emergency measure

- added five billion dollars for the elderly, blind, and disabled

- started the Legal Services Administration, which provides lawyers for the poor to fight landlords and loan sharks

- rushed our newest weapons to Israel when the Arabs attacked on Yom Kippur in 1973

- opened up relations with China
  (Well, we thought it was neat at the time.)

Nothing Richard Nixon did could make up for the fact that he nailed Alger Hiss, the urbane, handsome, impeccably dressed, high-level diplomat in the State Department with friends in high places, who turned out to be a spy for Russia. Nixon sent Hiss to prison—and liberals never forgave him.

"Tricky Dick" turned out to be a pretty popular president, to the dismay of those well-mannered liberals. He won a second term by a landslide. But the media took care of that—Watergate! A break-in at Democratic Party headquarters in Washington, DC. The *Washington Post* might have ignored if it had been another president, but this was Nixon. They pursued the crime on the front pages without letup until they undid the votes of millions and dispatched him from office.

It is clear that the media feels uneasy over what it did. Benghazi. Our ambassador and three other Americans murdered in a terrorist attack. But when clues began pointing to the president as the one who denied them help, the story practically disappeared from the news.

There was a brief item in the *New York Times* that said arms our president sent secretly to Qatar to go to the Libyan rebels went instead to al-Qaeda.

And another news item suggests that the rebels our president is supporting in Syria are linked to al-Qaeda.

None of this warrants further investigation, of course. Benghazi is no Watergate. And Obama is no Nixon.

Besides, you can't keep bringing down presidents. It's too embarrassing. And it could put you in the path of a drone which is considered by this government a legal way to kill American citizens deemed dangerous without benefit of a trial.

Attention Homeowners
New Recycling Schedule Effective Immediately

As a result of a breakdown of a new type of recycling truck that runs on a fuel just approved by the Department of Energy, we are required to adjust our recycling schedule. Kindly read and post in a prominent place. Forgetting can be costly.

On Mondays, you will put out the green container containing newsprint. The container must not overflow. If it does overflow, you must use a second green container or read fewer papers. Who reads newspapers nowadays anyhow?

On Tuesdays, you will put out the blue container containing glass bottles (not plastic). Please wash the bottles. There have been instances of our recycling engineers being splattered with tomato sauce. This does not help maintain a friendly relationship with them. Fines are being considered should such incidents continue.

On Wednesdays, you will put out the orange container containing plastic material. This includes plastic bottles, packaging, etc. The packaging must be washed out and flattened. Recycling engineers are not keen on sticking their hands into old lasagna. A fine will be imposed if contents are not washed. And it won't be a small one.

On Thursdays, you will put out the red container containing soft goods, usually cloth. This could be sheets, towels, flags, bandages, or whatever else you have. This would include used apparel, both men's and women's, with *buttons removed*. Buttons go in the orange container for plastic. Be sure that baby's discards are spanking clean, especially diapers. Poop must be flushed down toilets. Be careful, of course, not to flush the diaper down along with the poop. This can cause serious plumbing issues. And fines.

On Fridays, you will put out metal objects such as tin cans, paper clips, the zippers you removed from the soft goods that went out on Wednesday, as well as cutlery, metal plates, plaques, unwanted medals, and so on. *Do not include items such as old pencil sharpeners, toys, or manufactured goods. They are for the Saturday bin.*

On Saturdays, you will put out manufactured items as mentioned above, unless they are in working order, like old typewriters, which will not be accepted. You must donate them to Goodwill or some other nonsectarian recipient. We have many aspiring writers among the homeless who would appreciate your functioning Smith-Corona.

On Sundays, all containers must be out of sight. There will be roving inspectors. It is a good time to clean them for use the next week.

All recyclables must be out before 6:00 a.m. We do not want to repeat the incidents of recycling trucks blocking driveways at commuting hours, trapping people inside their garages and unable to get to work on time. Of course, we discourage cars and encourage use of public transportation. We might reconsider our blocking policy.

Thank you for your cooperation in making this a model recycling community. We must point out that under previous administrations—in the unaware preliberal Bush era—people were allowed to put out a garbage can or two and forget about it.

Not anymore—now we have rules.

We do regret the increased taxes required by enhanced recycling, but the tax will be levied only on the 1 percent among us with obscene incomes. You know who you are.

Next week you will receive the new mulch regulations.

We owe recycling to the environmentally aware liberals. Until they made it a cause, we just took out the garbage. Now it can be a criminal act. The funny thing is that recycling can add to pollution. Take newsprint, for instance. The additional plants and chemicals required to remove the print from the paper contaminate the rivers, which, in turn, require more chemicals and additional plants to purify. Not to mention energy used by all those waste management behemoths for their extra runs.

Here's a fun idea: sneak out at night and drop paper into your liberal neighbors' plastic bin, and a glass bottle into their paper bin. What a joy to read in the community press that they were taken from their home in handcuffs and have been sentenced to serve a year of weekends sorting garbage in the town dump.

You Know Who Your Enemies Are
Keep an Eye on Your Friends

—Posted on the wall of a charming
mosque outside of Sarajevo in the
recently created Muslim state of Bosnia

Whatever you feel about Muslims, you've got to admire a lot about their philosophy. It's sensible, practical, pragmatic, and filled with horse sense (or is that camel sense?). None of this "love thy neighbor" or "turn the other cheek" kind of thing. They know people. They know if you turn the other cheek you won't be thanked; you'll be considered a fool. They know you are decadent and immoral, yet think you're superior to them.

You can understand why they get enraged and maybe kill a few nuns when infidels insult their Koran.

They aren't casual about their religion, as many of us are. Their attitude toward religion is not church-only-on-special-holidays. They're under those domes bowing and praying every day—they *believe!*

And we'd better believe it.

Liberals, bless their hearts, love to see a charming mosque go up in the neighborhood. They love another opportunity to show how accepting they are. Forget that mosques are often centers where young men are recruited, indoctrinated, and trained to be terrorists. Liberals love to do exchange worshipping with our Muslim neighbors. You know, they come to our church or synagogue, and we go to their mosque. What a great way to promote mutual understanding.

After all, we are all brothers and sisters. What's past is past. It's time to share hummus and organic fries and forget a few isolated incidents that conservatives are politicizing.

If you don't share that point of view, you are no liberal.

Here's a cool strategy for closet conservatives. At your next book club meeting, instead of reading the latest Oprah recommendation, suggest that the group read the Koran. What a revelation it will turn out to be. Not only will your liberal, intellectual friends love the idea of being enlightened, but it will also cement your credentials as being one of them. And instead of the usual luncheon sandwiches, bring halal* food and pita bread.

The women might want to wear headscarves.

And walk obediently behind the men.

---

* Saad Fayed, "Halal Food," About.com/odj/middleeasternfood101. *Halal* in Arabic means permitted. Halal foods are those allowed under Islamic dietary guidelines.

"The Politics of Personal Destruction"
—Sarah Palin

As a closet conservative, you'll be doing some of your most important reading in the closet.

You'll angle your Kindle on the train or plane to cause excruciating neck kinks in case anyone seated next to you tries to sneak a peak. Liberals do that. They've got KGB in their blood. You'll want to have a false book jacket at the ready—something neutral like *The Diversity of Protons* so no one will ask what you are reading.

The last thing you want to do is get caught reading a book by Sarah Palin—top target of the liberal attack machine. In her book, *Going Rogue: An American Life*, she calls it "the politics of personal destruction," a phrase she oddly shares with Bill Clinton who claimed it during his impeachment. An impeachment that ended, while Palin's never stops. The attacks continue from TV talk panels and Hollywood starlets showing their smarts.

Palin is one of the most accomplished women in the country. She was governor of Alaska. Vice presidential nominee. As governor, she destroyed a corrupt political machine. She was courageous, independent, and admired. But the moment she gave that speech at the Republican National Convention, she was a marked woman. The media portray her as a dimwit. Her family is spied upon. Stories are made up. Anything goes.

The first thing liberals do is try to get the goods on you, she says, even if they have to invent them. Affairs. Tax dodges. Drinking. Drugs. Racism. They'll seek out your elementary school class to see if they can get you on bullying the fat kid in the sixth grade. They'll seek out a rejected lover or a disgruntled employee. Twist the facts. Turn your love for a retarded child into a selfish political ploy.

Liberals made Bain Capital the enemy rather than a creator of businesses. They'll come up with an Anita Hill. George Bush, of course, was a draft dodger and drunk driver. Forget his achievements in Texas. If Mitt Romney's taxes seem low, don't mention the fortune he gives to charities that lowers his income.

Whatever it takes to win, do it. After all, you aren't being ruthless for yourself, but to save the country from the pickup-truck people.

No wonder Palin went rogue when John McCain would not bring up Obama's twenty-year intimacy with the America-hating, Jew-hating, white-hating Reverend Jeremiah Wright. Why shouldn't voters know about Obama's terrorist pals in Chicago? she asked. Like Bernadine Dohrn, who killed a police officer. Her husband, Bill Ayers, is to this day a terrorist pal of Obama's who Colin Powell, apparently a closeted democrat all the years he was being advanced by Republicans, dismisses as some guy from Chicago. McCain was too nice to do attack politics, even if it meant letting people know the truth. And we know what happens to nice guys.

Sarah Palin knew.

But she didn't read the right papers.

So stay calm when you hear: *Hey, Sarah, what about those reports of your involvement with a state trooper? Or Todd's hanky-panky with your hairdresser in Wassilla? You know, Myrt the Flirt.*

What can we closet conservatives do about it?

How about: "I hear that Nancy Pelosi's nickname in high school was "Nancy No-Pantsy." And Harry Reid was called "Harry the Fairy" in college. You might mention one of these loudly in Grand Central Station, and then duck into the crowd. Or while waiting at the baggage carousel at the airport where no one knows you. You'll think of others.

Rodney King Day
Let's Get the Bill through Congress Now.
Give Him the Honor He Deserves!

Close the schools. Lower the flag. Rodney King died. He was found dead at the bottom of his swimming pool. He was forty-seven years old. A hero to liberals. He was pursued on a Los Angeles freeway by the racist police as he wove in and out of traffic at one hundred miles per hour. He resisted arrest and was beaten into submission. The beating was caught on police video and broadcast around the world. The police, not King, were put on trial and found *innocent*.

A week of rioting followed and miles of Los Angeles were destroyed. The officers were retried and liberals got the verdict they wanted. The bad cops went to jail (cops are always bad), while King was freed (pocketing a few million dollars from the city), ending up as the star attraction at the Democratic convention.

Later, as the radio and television interviews dwindled, King was in and out of jail for indiscretions like assault, drunkenness, even dangerous driving. He beat up a few girlfriends. Took drugs. The usual ghetto stuff. But he will remain a liberal hero forever.

Oh, how wonderful those days of glory were when King demonstrated that a black man could be rewarded and become a celebrity for breaking the white man's racist laws! And the fiasco let cops everywhere know they were being watched.

Drive carefully.

Directions to My House

Take the Martin Luther King Jr. Freeway to Martin Luther King Jr. Avenue. After a mile, turn left onto Martin Luther King Jr. Boulevard. Go straight to Martin Luther King Jr. Road. Turn left at Martin Luther King Jr. Street. Follow to the end and turn onto Martin Luther King Jr. Lane. Be careful not to go to either Martin Luther King Jr. Circle, Martin Luther King Jr. Drive, or Martin Luther King Jr. Court. We're on Martin Luther King Jr. *Lane*.

They are planning to rename the bridge in our town the Martin Luther King Jr. Bridge. It is just across from the Martin Luther King Jr. Park. As for the library, the lead name right now is Zora Neale Hurston. Also in contention are James Baldwin and Richard Wright.

You might think there are many African Americans in our town. Actually, there is just a handful. But we certainly wish there were more. The high school kids are planning a Kwanzaa party, however, as a symbol of togetherness. The smart-ass who suggested they all come in blackface was severely reprimanded.

Martin Luther King Jr. is the only American who has his own holiday. Washington and Lincoln once did, but we have combined those into Presidents' Day—that takes care of the lot. Some reactionaries have suggested we bring those guys back and give them their own days—after all, George Washington did get this country going. But remember those slaves he owned. And others have pumped for Eisenhower, would you believe? Those right-wingers never give up.

Bush did it.
But not well.

Thank the Lord for Rednecks
They're the Only Ones We Can Still Offend

Here's a little secret about liberals. Since they are forbidden to ridicule blacks, Muslims, Jews, Asians, women, Catholics, nerds, fat people, and retards, they hang around the club and tell redneck jokes. (*Rednecks* are called so because their necks get sunburned when they work in the fields, heads bent.) Rednecks talk funny, drive pickups and know how to fix 'em, and they like the opposite sex or animals. They smoke, believe people should work for a living, don't want mosques in their towns, and lately they vote Republican. Here are some thigh-slappers to break the ice at Ethical Culture coffees:

Ways to Tell You're a Redneck

Your boat hasn't left the driveway in fifteen years.

You think the stock market has a fence around it.

You keep a can of Raid on the kitchen table.

You think a subdivision is part of a math problem.

You go to a family reunion to pick up women.

The neighbors have started a petition over your barking dog.

None of your shirts cover your stomach.

Your screen door has no screen.

You think the last words to "The Star-Spangled Banner" are *play ball.*

Bush likes country music.
If only he could figure out how to get his iPod to work.

We're Just Wild about Harry

To liberals, the most glorious election in history was the 1948 miracle, when bumbling Harry Truman—written off as a sure loser—defeated New York Governor Thomas Dewey, one of the most qualified presidential candidates ever.

Feisty Harry launched a whistle-stop campaign, riding a train to every town in the country. He stood at the back and spoke with confidence and enthusiasm in a thin voice and Missouri twang. Millions of people—who had never seen a live president—rushed to see him and vote for him. He won.

Suddenly, everybody was wild about Harry. He went on to get us into the Korean War in which six hundred thousand Americans were killed. It took the next president, Eisenhower, to end the war, leaving the boundaries exactly where they had been when the young men were alive. That's something we don't hear much about.

We still love Harry because he played poker with the boys, was a henpecked husband with a dreadful wife, and was a loving father who lashed out at a critic who suggested his singing daughter pursue another career (which she did, writing successful Washington-based mystery stories).

Dark horse straight-talk henpecked Harry won, and was now adored by the American public. With the exception of the families of the six hundred thousand boys who lay buried in military cemeteries.

Who can forget the front-page picture of Lauren Bacall sitting atop a piano, shapely legs swinging, while a grinning Harry sat at the keyboard playing the "Missouri Waltz"? He did not miss a beat as he eyed her dangling legs.

Nixon played the piano too. But the only movie star the Republicans had was John Wayne. And he didn't do piano-top sitting.

Racism Is Dead
Don't Tell Anyone

One of the best kept secrets in the country is that racism is dead. Yes, kaput. Gone—bye-bye. There is no job an African American can't get, no school he can't get into, no neighborhood off limits, no profession he can't enter, and no political office he can't hold, including the presidency. So what's going on?

A top priority among liberals is to keep racism alive. And only liberals are fighting it. Lose the threat of racism and you lose a huge voting bloc. A black kid gets shot breaking into a Nike store. *Racism.* A black man tries to jimmy open his front door and a suspicious cop stops him. *Racism.* A stop-and-frisk program turns up high numbers of blacks carrying concealed weapons. *Racism.* There are far more blacks than whites in prison. *Racism.* More whites than blacks have higher paying jobs. *Racism.* It's too good to give up even when it no longer exists.

The days of Hattie McDaniel, *The Amos 'n Andy Show*, and Stepin Fetchit ("Feets, do your stuff!") are long gone. Today Denzel Washington is a star. Not to mention Oprah Winfrey.

Liberals love to point out that our country was founded by white, male slave owners. This, of course, makes everything we do a little racist. (Does this mean that nonwhite males who did *not* own slaves weren't as smart as the other guys?)

They say the March of Dimes people went ballistic when a vaccine was discovered that wiped out polio and their jobs. No slouches, they came up with an even better affliction—birth defects. All the dimes in the world will not cure that one.

No matter how many laws are passed, no matter that our biggest television personalities are black, no matter that our president is black, and that even some Republicans are black, liberals are going to keep racism alive.

They have found the incurable dream.

If the People Who Write the Movies You See Hate the United States and Love Communist Russia, Wouldn't You Want to Know It?

Not If You're a Liberal

When the right-wingers went after the Hollywood Ten, who did the media support?

The Hollywood Ten—ten highly paid, influential screenwriters and directors who would not say whether or not they were members of the Communist Party. They "took the Fifth," a popular phrase at the time, referring to the neat amendment in our constitution that gives you the right to remain silent if telling the truth can be awkward. It turns catching criminals into a kind of game.

These were all successful, talented men who looked a lot better, spoke a lot more cleverly, and thought they knew a lot more than those hick congressmen in baggy suits who persecuted them.

So what if their sympathies were with one of the most brutal governments of all time? That was capitalist propaganda. They knew the truth. Liberals always know. So they cleverly slipped their ideology into the movies we saw. Stars like Ginger Rogers and Ronald Reagan found themselves appearing in films that showed the United States at its worst.* You would have thought that the Klan ran the southern states—the rich were selfish fools who lived in swank Park Avenue apartments, indifferent to the poor in tenements who were driven to crime by hard-hearted bankers and steel magnates.

But something happened.

They were discovered. They were investigated. And many were blacklisted, unable to get jobs simply because they were working for the enemy. Many of the writers continued to turn in manuscripts in plain manila envelopes under assumed names.

But it blew over, and the Hollywood Ten quietly returned. And multiplied.

Today, it's the pro-American writers and directors who are blacklisted.

---

* *Storm Warning* (1951) starring Ginger Rogers, Ronald Reagan, and Doris Day shows a typical American town run by the Ku Klux Klan.

Slavery's Been Abolished?
You're Kidding

The liberals have managed to keep slavery a red-hot guilt issue, even though it ended a hundred and fifty years ago. The Emancipation Proclamation was issued in 1863. Six hundred thousand Americans died in the Civil War.

But slavery is too good to give up.

It's one of those vote-getting issues liberals keep alive, like abortion rights that have survived both Republican and Democratic administrations, but sages like Scarlett Johansson feel are in immediate danger.

In liberal America, the darkies are still picking cotton, and Simon Legree is still snapping his whip. If someone says what a great country this is, liberals reply, "What about slavery?"

When our founding fathers are praised for creating a democracy after the revolution—rather than the usual tyranny that follows—liberals reply that they were white men who owned slaves. Two crimes.

When the United States is praised as the first nation whose constitution declares that all men are created equal, liberals say *what about Thomas Jefferson's slaves?*

Keep this under your hat, but it seems to me that American blacks should be grateful for slavery. If their ancestors hadn't been brought here one way or another, they would be living in countries like Rwanda, Nigeria, and Somalia, where people get massacred seasonally.

We just might mention to our liberal friends that the Republican Party came into being to *end* slavery, and succeeded. Say that with a smirk, of course, or you'll be suspect.

I See England, I See France,
I See Teacher's Underpants
Teacher, Teacher, I Declare,
I Can See Your Underwear

In the days when conservatives were in charge, children were unhealthily repressed. The only way they could express their feelings was in giggling taunts uttered out of hearing distance. Today, thanks to progressive education and organizations championing Children's Rights, kids let their feelings out. They attack teachers. Erasers can be deadly. Child psychologists and other experts now fill the schools. They deal with "real feelings." Children who are dangerous, of course, go off to special classes with specially educated teachers. And police on hand. Good preparation for serving time. Of course, school budgets have soared.

According to a letter from a teacher in the *Wall Street Journal*, government mandates are issued regularly on educating children with diagnosed disabilities—physical, emotional, learning, and so on—as well as children who can't speak English.* She says that "schools are required

---

* Andrew Coulson, "America Has Too Many Teachers," *Wall Street Journal*, July 10, 2012.

to have social workers, speech and language teachers, psychologists, PE teachers, technology teachers, driver's education teachers, early-childhood teachers, night-school teachers, summer school teachers, etc."

So you see, you people who live in the past, schools are no longer places where children learn the three Rs. They are dedicated to developing the whole child so that when they go out into the world, no child is left behind.

Whoops—I didn't really mean to say that to a liberal.

Lynch Those Uppity Blacks Who Don't Know the Meaning of Gratitude

The one turncoat liberals will never forgive is that ingrate on the Supreme Court, Clarence Thomas.

Would you believe that an African American who grows up poor and oppressed in the segregated South and goes to Yale as a result of affirmative action then ends up *opposing* affirmative action? He claims that after receiving a law degree and a load of honors, it was tough to get a job.

Potential employers eye us warily, Thomas says, suspecting it is color rather than ability that gets us our diplomas. The first employer who looked at him as Clarence Thomas and not as a black man—he says in his autobiography—was Missouri Senator John Danforth.

He appointed Thomas assistant attorney general of Missouri. Yes, Missouri.

George Bush the First nominated him for the Supreme Court. This drove the liberals crazy—a rightist African American who thought for himself and left the plantation. They set out to destroy Thomas any way they could. Since they could not stop him on qualification grounds, they got an ideological black woman who once worked for Thomas to scream sexual harassment. Not the sharpest tool in the shed, Anita Hill had some trouble keeping her story consistent. Thomas made it to the bench, and Hill became the star of the women's movement.

She was the guest speaker at a number of important lunches, she appeared on television talk shows where the hosts could not stop bowing, and she accepted a job offer from Brandeis University. Here she joined another liberal icon, cop killer Bernadine Dorhn, the wife of Obama's longtime friend Bill Ayers.

Can you blame the liberals for being miffed? I mean, after all they have done for his kind. Welfare. Aid to dependent children. Public housing. Food stamps. Affirmative action. Busing. Liberals have given black people everything—including Detroit. They are entitled to gratitude.

Or it's the whip.

(Did you know that a higher percentage of Republicans than Democrats voted for the Civil Rights Bill? But we all know that when Republicans do something good, it's because they have to. Democrats do something good because they *want* to.)

Would you believe the Democrats asked me to their convention? I would have gone, but I lost the damn RSVP.

You think maybe Laura threw it out?

If His Mother Had Listened to Planned Parenthood, Steve Jobs Might Not Have Died of Cancer
He Might Never Have Lived

Urged to abort, the unmarried young woman, pregnant with the future Steve Jobs, chose to have her baby and give him up for adoption. He grew up tormented by the fact that he had been given away. His behavior was often considered weird. He had abrupt outbursts and lashed out at the people closest to him. The reports are endless of his viciousness toward the employees of Pixar and Apple, his betrayals of friends and lovers, and his unpredictable rebuffing of those closest to him.*

Even as he gave the world all those *i*'s—iMac, iPhone, iPod, and iPads—he was a troubled man who often suffered physical and emotional pain. He was haunted until the day he died by the knowledge that he had been unwanted. He died after a grueling battle with cancer.

Steve Jobs would have been spared all of this if his mother had simply gone to Planned Parenthood and had one of the easy-does-it abortions they are said to perform regularly. But Jobs's mother caved to the right-to-lifers, and Steve Jobs suffered with that decision all his life.

Despite opposition from us "war on women" Republicans, the government regularly ups the money it grants Planned Parenthood to prevent another slipup like Steve Jobs.

---

* Walter Isaacson, *Steve Jobs* (New York: Simon & Schuster, 2011).

Barney Frank Gets Married to a Man Twenty-Five Years Younger

Nancy Pelosi Does the Shimmy

Senator John Kerry and Governor Deval Patrick Leave Early *Together*

It's a liberal's dream. The first congressional gay wedding. A famous congressman becomes the wife of a good-looking younger man, a florist who works out. And Barney Frank is no ordinary congressman. As head of the congressional Finance Committee, he oversaw the running of Fannie

Mae and Freddie Mac into the ground when they were guaranteeing all those subpar mortgages.

When straight guys warned that those mortgages were not being repaid and that government agencies backing them were in danger of collapse, Frank told them to buzz off. Convinced that homeownership would make people responsible citizens, Fannie Mae continued giving away homes with no down payment and monthly payments so low they were laughable.

Alas, the warnings proved true. The new "homeowners" did not turn into responsible citizens; rather, they ignored the monthly payments until they were evicted and then ran off with the appliances. So the housing bubble burst and the country is reeling. But all's well that ends well. Barney Frank is married to the man he loves. The homophobic right-wingers are saying *screw Barney Frank*, but that's being handled already.

Progressives hope that this is just the beginning of same-sex politicians exchanging vows at the altar. Wouldn't it be cool if the next chupa-dupa had two women beaming at each other? How about Elena Kagan and Sonia Sotomayor? Two Supreme Court justices!

Catch me—I'm fainting.

Would You Believe Those Insensitive Right-Wingers Tried to Put Grandma in a Dump?
The Dump War in Paradise

Paradise is an enclave of lovely homes in Westchester, New York, outnumbered by the town's mostly blue-collar houses. The opulent Tudor-style houses are homes to mostly wealthy Jewish people dedicated to liberal causes—freedom of choice, recycling, civil rights, and integration. People like us with different views blend in silently; the only indication we are the enemy is the *Wall Street Journal* flung on our driveways instead of the *New York Times.*

Surrounding Paradise is a much greater number of working-class houses inhabited by plumbers, painters, barbers, and handymen who elect the local politicians. The two groups pretend to like each other even after the Dump War.

Here is how the Dump War began:

The federal government gave the town a grant with instructions to build public housing for elderly minority women. Such decrees come regularly from one bureau or another in Washington.

On examining the latest edict, we realized that nothing would prevent the grandchildren of these low-income minority women from living with them. This would include teenage grandchildren who might be sporting tattoos and nose rings, and whose behavior might call for extra police. This type of housing is usually built in the downscale part of towns where people own pit bulls. Liberals are all for it.

Not this time.

Our mayor, the owner of an auto repair shop, announced with a cunning smile that for the building site, the town had chosen some vacant land on the edge of Paradise, long used as a dump. Screened from view by trees, it was used mostly for leaves, logs, clippings, and an occasional discarded bicycle or scooter, which would quickly disappear. Past the screened dump were carefully maintained clay tennis courts, which required a permit, a key, and correct clothing to enter. A few steps beyond and you are in Paradise.

Funny, instead of welcoming this opportunity to live their convictions, the liberals in Paradise were enraged. They didn't fear drugs, rape, muggings, or graffiti—instead they worried about the health of these poor women living on what could have been toxic land. These women, who had already been through so much, deserved better.

Paradise had an abundance of lawyers, chemical engineers, and activist women who rushed into action. Phone calls, e-mails, text messages. There was meeting after meeting. Soil experts, engineers, and chemists bumped into each other at the dump as multiple environmental impact studies were conducted. They eventually came up with what they were looking for. The dump where no chemicals had ever been deposited turned out to be lethal. To expose elderly women to it would be a death sentence. The price of making it safe was prohibitive.

Today, elderly minority women live happily in a lovely project in an uncontaminated area near the railroad tracks. An environmental study found it absolutely safe. And the controversial dump has been preserved as open space for the liberal residents of Paradise who welcomed the newcomers to their new home near the tracks with a donation to buy pit bulls.

Hillary almost lived here

You can imagine the joy in Paradise when Hillary Clinton was spotted there with a real estate agent. She was in search of a home that would make her a resident of New York so she could run for senator. It was one of several Westchester communities she was scouting—all wealthy and white. No one seemed to question why this woman who was such an advocate of integration didn't even glance at one of our diverse communities. She sped through them with windows raised as if terrorists were pursuing her.

Bush did it.

Again.

Chappa What?
Look, Accidents Will Happen

Senator Ted Kennedy died in 2009.

This liberal icon was given a funeral the sultan of Bahrain would have envied. Not a word about Chappaquiddick or Mary Jo Kopechne—those unfortunate mishaps that only right-wingers made a big deal of. Liberals, on the other hand, are sensitive and forgiving. They have cornered the market on compassion. They are loyal to one another right to the jailhouse door. They put their party above their country.

So what if the White House is filled with leaks? Too bad about that doctor who helped us get Osama bin Laden. So he'll die in a Pakistani jail. And tough about those four Americans, including our ambassador, killed in Benghazi because Obama denied them aid. You don't want to get the goods on a Democratic president even if it looks like he's working for the enemy.

Republicans crossed over to work with Democrats to oust Nixon—something about the *good of the country.*

Congressman Barney Frank. If he were a Republican like Mark Foley, he would have been drummed out of congress for his gay activities. Not *our* Barney. So what if he used his influence to fix traffic tickets for the male prostitute living with him? Barney came back stronger than ever. He was made head of the House Financial Services Committee that oversaw Fannie Mae and Freddie Mac as they collapsed. He clearly had better things to oversee.

Look at Charles Rangel, a New York congressman who failed to report taxable income from property he secretly owned. And Bill Clinton. Look what those jealous Republicans tried to do to *him*. He came back stronger than ever. Jesse Jackson. Even Martin Luther King was said to have a few cookies on the side.

The point is *if you're planning to break the law, civil or moral, be a liberal.*

Always Look for the Indian Cemetery
And You Can Stop Anything

Right-wingers, as liberals know, don't give a fig for the environment, public safety, human rights, historical preservation, nature, or the arts. When we see empty space, we want to build on it. When we see land, we want to frack it. When we breathe clean air, we want to pollute it. When we see water, we want to kill all the fish. This is why liberals would like to see us leave the planet.

When Woody Allen was about to have his view blocked by a high-rise, he summoned his liberal friends and the block was landmarked. Not so much as a brick can be touched, let alone a building leveled, to make way for a new one. Ever since a slave cemetery was discovered when excavating for a skyscraper in lower Manhattan, archeological digs are mandatory before a building permit is issued. All across the country developers have been sacrificed for sacred sites.

In southern Florida, the I-95 highway makes a bend that cost millions of extra dollars to pave and requires extra miles of driving, all to save an insect. (You will find no footnote because all records have been expunged, and the workers are rumored to have been buried in the asphalt.) But there are living witnesses who will confirm this when you ask why in the world you have to make an endless loop around nothing when a straight road would make more sense.

The Bella Abzug[*] award goes to the dedicated lady who led an eleven-year fight against the most powerful politicians and interests in New York to stop the building of Westway, a proposed elevated highway meant to circle Manhattan with miles of new parkland below. She rallied troops of West Side mothers pushing baby carriages, and oddball intellectuals who believe all cars belong in California, and she succeeded.

---

[*] Bella Abzug," *Wikipedia,* last modified January 14, 2013, http://en.wikipedia.org/wiki/Bella_Abzug. Bella Abzug, nicknamed Battling Bella, was a Bronx, New York congresswoman from 1973-1977. She was known for her big hats, staunch liberalism, and abrasiveness. When asked why Abzug lost her own district in her last bid for Congress, Mayor Koch said, "Her neighbors know her."

This turned out to be a blessing. *(Excuse the expression, liberals.)* The predicted traffic tie-ups did not happen. Much of the traffic mysteriously disappeared. Sometimes people are *right* who claim that the more roads you build the more traffic there is. We conservatives are the first to admit we are wrong—which to liberals, alas, is a sign of weakness.

The Kennedy family owned an estate by the ocean in Palm Beach. You might remember it as the scene of various rape charges and other high jinks. But when the Kennedys put it up for sale (at the height of the housing boom, coincidentally), they found no one would buy it since it was landmarked. A designation of its historical significance prevented anyone from making changes—like installing air conditioning. That would have required some architectural blasphemy.

What to do? You take away its landmark designation. For most people, that would entail lawyers and appeals. But the Kennedys did it with a phone call.

You can see it today, if you can recognize it after all the changes.

A half-dozen ugly Walmarts (to a liberal there is no such thing as an attractive Walmart) were stopped in the Southwest when flint tools and funny-looking carvings came up with the earth. They were declared to be authentic religious figures by experts in such matters—and the owners of tourist shops in the area promptly raised their prices on plastic replicas rushed in from China.

They are also sold in the Walmarts that opened not far away, after the chain reportedly contributed to various foundations to preserve Native American culture.

Buried authentic Indian artifact …

Watch out, Home Depot.

What Do We Get for the Blank Check We Sign to the United Nations?
Meals at Five-Star Restaurants and Free Parking Spaces in New York City

One of the things you don't do in our liberal world is criticize the UN. Liberals adore it. It has survived charges of corruption, waste, malfeasance, incompetence, and Hurricane Sandy. (The UN building was one of the safest places to be in partially flooded Manhattan.) Where would the world be without it?

Who do you think has kept Syria from exploding? *Special UN forces.*

Who do you think has kept a watchful eye on Hamas while it imports weapons from Iran and lobs missiles into Israel daily? *Special UN forces.*

Who do you think has overseen human rights throughout the world?

UN members like Rwanda, Zimbabwe, and Somalia—where people who don't know when to keep their mouths shut disappear forever.

And who has the courage to condemn Israel? Isn't it important to hear the voices of Castro, Chavez, Assad, and the president of Iran? How else will we come to an understanding? Do we really know the Holocaust was not a Jewish plot to grab Palestine? Or that there really *was* a Holocaust?

Liberals listen to all points of view that tell us how bad we are. They are thrilled to have the Taliban speak at our universities. And roll out the Persian carpet for Muslim dignitaries, who entertain our journalists at lavish UN receptions where they tell us the real history of Islam that embraces peace and tolerance.

They can't believe that we conservatives want the United States to stop funding the UN. To quote a Harvard-educated delegate: "Off with their heads." Or at least their hands.

Worm Rights
We Liberals Care

Worms don't rank high on the list of endangered species, but the time to act is while they are still hale and hearty. The first thing we have to do is get laws passed banning the use of worms as bait. What could be crueler than impaling a live worm on a hook and plunging it into the water to be devoured? That is so Republican. There is no reason artificial lures can't be mandatory. For people who can't afford them, we'll have government subsidies. The application forms are already being written. As for the unfortunate expression, "The early bird gets the worm," we will expunge it from our early-education readers and reprimand anyone caught saying it. It not only encourages indifference to worm life, but also it sends the wrong message. It values striving and competitiveness, when what we want instead is cooperation, equality, and sharing. Otherwise, the 1 percent will end up with all the worms.

How to Pass as a Liberal
Take This Quick Test

You are a liberal if...

When you are requested to show identification at the polls and have none, you cry "racism" if you are black, then you threaten to call the Reverend Jeremiah Wright (reported to be under house arrest since Obama first ran). Otherwise, you show your driver's license, and you vote.

You major in Minority Studies and when you can't get a job anywhere except Chick-fil-A or Walmart, you go to the ACLU or the NAACP. You can't understand why your knowledge of Harriet Tubman* makes no impression on executives concerned with algorithms.

If you want to vote for your candidate more than once, you go to ACORN. Closely connected with Obama, his friends there will fix you up.

---

* Harriet Tubman was an escaped slave who made nineteen trips back to the South to bring other slaves out—starting the "Underground Railroad." Born in slavery in 1820, she died free in 1913 (www.harriettubmanbiograpy.com).

Your heroes are Jesse Jackson, Al Sharpton, Hillary and Bill, Barack and Michelle, Nancy Pelosi, Harry Reid, Warren Buffet, Al "Jazeera" Gore, Katie Couric, and the leaker who turned in the Pakistani doctor who helped us get Bin Laden and is now spending the rest of his life in a Pakistan jail.

If the winter is bitterly cold, you say that the Republicans will use this to deny global warming. If it's unseasonably hot, you say something scornful about the Republicans denying global warming.

You despise the Tea Party, laugh at Sarah Palin, and agree that the Occupiers have a legitimate gripe. Defecating on the sidewalks is a smart way to get your grievances noticed when you carry a sign saying "Shit on the 1 percent."

You think it's only right that all the stadiums at the U. S. Open are named for African Americans. Even though Louis Armstrong couldn't hit a backhand to save his life.

You get livid at gas-guzzling SUVs, which are mostly filled with big families. People shouldn't have all those children anyway; it's bad for the earth.

You condemn fracking that would give us energy independence because it makes a mess of the landscape nobody ever cared much about anyhow.

Although the last thing you are is racist, you believe as a liberal that African Americans are incapable of taking care of themselves, and will starve to death if the government does not provide them with everything required to stay alive.

You don't mention that Al Gore has turned into a blimp, catching up to Michael Moore. But you howl at Governor Christie.

You exchange raised eyebrows when Richard Nixon is mentioned, assuming everyone in the room hates him as much as you are expected to.
The same with Ronald Reagan.

When the conversation turns to bad countries, you immediately condemn the United States for putting Japanese Americans in concentration camps during World War II. And for lynchings in the South. And for starvation wages for grape pickers. Well, yes, Hitler and Stalin did some mean things too.

You say it was the Republicans who made President Roosevelt send ships of Jewish refugees back to Hitler's Germany to be gassed. Funny, this president who won four terms, and was the most popular president in history, was suddenly powerless against those anti-Semites who could barely carry a state.

You believe we are all owed free contraceptives and the best medical attention—no matter how much we smoke, drink, or have unprotected sex with whomever.

You believe we must not profile even if that is the surest way to stop crime. *(Don't breathe this to a soul, but if I were a member of a high-crime group, I would be glad to be profiled—I would feel safer, not indignant.)*

You are opposed to waterboarding, no matter how many terrorists it has turned into fountains of information.

You call the Cleveland Indians the *Cleveland Native Americans*. And the Black Bottom dance is the *African American Bottom*.

You believe the purpose of schools is to teach children to get along with one another and have lots of sex with a variety of partners. If you can't do that, what good are reading, writing, and higher mathematics? (Worse, you will be unprepared for Sex Week at Yale.)

You never raise your voice to a child. You might crush her self-esteem. You use reason when she threatens to hurl a $250 doll at the glass case at American Girl. (Which means you should buy her the doll.) Maybe you can hold back on some accessories.

You believe we must search all airline passengers with equal vigor. We can't offend the most likely terrorists by not groping everyone. Which, I suspect, some legislators enjoy.

You can't play Frisbee in your yard anymore. It is filled with recycling containers.

You are pro-choice when it comes to abortions, but not when it comes to schools. All schools offer *some* benefits. Private schools may provide more academics, but your child will never learn how to take down a mugger, which could prove to be a lifesaving skill. There are definite advantages to public schools in dangerous neighborhoods. Appreciate them.

You believe that if Martha Stewart sells stock because her broker informs her that other clients are selling, she should go to jail. But if a disadvantaged youth murders a classmate for his sneakers, give him counseling.

How to Be an Outsider in
Our Liberal World
Say What You Think

I was a liberal once. My friends were liberal. To be anything else was unthinkable. But that chip in my brain had a short. I started to notice disturbing things, like criminals having more rights than victims. The unqualified replacing the qualified. Busing turning schools into terror camps. My taxes rising without mercy, along with welfare rolls. It hit me that I was on the wrong side.

I shared my revelation with friends, assuming they would be interested. Mistake. I was the Benedict Arnold of our suburb. A friend stood up at a dinner party at our house, rang his glass, and announced, "It shows how dumb the American people are. They voted for Reagan twice."

He looked at me as he sat down and said, "I know you voted for Reagan."

After spending an evening with a couple we had known for years, during which time they ridiculed Rudolph Giuliani, Clarence Thomas, Sarah Palin, Dick Cheney, and the Bushes without the slightest concern for our feelings, Chuck shook my hand in the driveway and said, "We like you anyway, even if you are Republicans."

Chuck owned a remodeling business that would not let African Americans answer the phones for fear it would be known as a black company.

When I made my regular we're-going-to-Florida good-bye call to a friend of many years, I mentioned that I had learned about America on our drives to Florida. We stopped in different towns—not just at highway motels—and got to know people and some southern history. There was a pause on his end after which he said, "Oh yes, the red states."

I kiddingly replied that I was pretty much a red stater myself. "I can't take this anymore," he said, and hung up.

Apparently nothing else in our relationship had mattered in all the years we had known each other. I was one of the bad guy conservatives. Funny, I had no problem with his being an immovable Democrat. It was okay with me if he admired Jesse Jackson, although I couldn't understand why.

I cannot tell you how many times on the tennis court I hear jokes about Sarah Palin, George Bush, and Rudy Giuliani from New York liberals who assume I feel as they do. They never mention Obama's reverence for the Reverend Wright, or Benghazi, but they sneer at John McCain, who refused to be released from a Vietnamese prison camp without his buddies.

I even kept silent on 9/11, when the news came that planes were attacking the World Trade Center and my tennis partner said, "This will give Bush an excuse to increase military spending." People were jumping from windows.

Look, if you're going to get into games, you've got to play the game.

Let's Hear It for the
Forgotten Liberal Hero

Walter Duranty was the Moscow Bureau Chief of the *New York Times* from 1922 to 1936. An enthusiastic supporter of the new Russian society, he withheld news of famine and purges, substituting instead stories that praised the supposed accomplishments of the Communist regime.

It was more important, he and the *New York Times* felt, to gain support for this bold new government of the people than to report the truth. As a result, readers of the *New York Times* (many of the most influential people in America) knew very little of the gulags, the executions, or the mass famines in the Soviet Union—but they knew a lot about the blossoming of the ideal society. If the liquidations were mentioned, they were justified. If opponents of Stalin disappeared, it was not reported.

There was no space for negativism among the articles devoted to the joy of working in factories run by the people. Readers learned about the wonderful state health plan and free vacations for workers on the Baltic beaches, but not about lining up to buy food. Or getting shot.

The *New York Times* actually apologized years later for their selective journalism. There was even talk of withdrawing the Pulitzer Prize given to Duranty for his dishonest reporting, but it was decided to forget about it. His reports, after all, were beautifully written. And his motives were good. He was an idealist trying to help create a better world for all of us.

Karl Marx

I sometimes wonder if Alger Hiss and the other Communist sympathizers in our state department—intellectuals who read the *New York Times* faithfully, as people do today—would have thought and acted differently if the newspaper that helped shape their worldview had written the truth.

You might ask this question of your liberal friends, but with caution.

"I know vouchers would help us and the Republicans are for that, but I'm a Democrat and I vote Democrat."
—Spoken by an African American lady to a reporter on Michigan Boulevard in Chicago

That's where liberals have it way over us righties. Loyalty. It's like they have a chip embedded in their brains with all political views programmed for life.

They are programmed to believe that Republicans are the party of the rich. That we conservatives are tall, blond, smiling people with perfect teeth who belong to exclusive clubs, play polo, live in all-white communities, show dogs, play excellent golf and tennis, and have no concern at all for those other people except when we're at charity balls.

Liberals know there's a catch to whatever righties propose to benefit the common people. All this talk about wanting them to be responsible is an excuse to end welfare and throw them in the streets. Whatever we do for Israel, we are labeled anti-Semitic. Nixon might have saved the Jewish state at its most perilous hour and Golda Meir might have adored him, but American Jews voted for the guy with the "D" after his name. Obama supports the rise of the Muslim Brotherhood in Egypt, and Jews stick by him. Go figure.

We know it's the Republican Party that came into being to end slavery. And that more Republicans than Democrats voted for the Civil Rights Bill—but the liberals grabbed the credit. Minorities know it's the Democrats who give them aid for dependent children, affirmative action, public housing, and government jobs, and who kowtow to them at every election. It's that chip.

"We aren't going to be tricked by their vouchers and charter schools. We know it's a plan to take money away from public schools and leave us all in the lurch. So whatever those Repubs propose, no matter how good it sounds, deep down we know they're up to something," says that lady on Michigan Boulevard on the steps of the public library. "I've already made up my mind. Don't confuse me with the facts."

You can't ever trust a Republican.
There's a couple over there.

It Pays to Have Friends in High Places

See the Muslim Brotherhood
celebrating its victory in Cairo.
The Muslim Brotherhood now rules Egypt.
Hamas is an offshoot of the Muslim Brotherhood.
Hamas fires missiles into Israel, straps
explosives around their children's bodies,
and sends them off to bliss.
President Obama has just added another
billion to the billions we give Egypt.
Could that mean that American
taxpayers are now funding Hamas?

What happened?

If you want to keep your liberal friends, you won't ask.

The Bible
It Isn't Entirely Useless

Liberals aren't big on Bible study. In fact, keeping religion out of our lives is a number-one priority. No crèches, Christmas trees, stars of David, or angels on public property. They don't exactly go around quoting scripture. Except for one: *Love Thine Enemy*.

They think Hugo Chavez has a lot going for him. After all, he hates America. Che Guevara is their hero. Never mind that a few thousand Cubans were tortured to death. Ya gotta admire Fidel. He really let the Cuban professional and middle classes have it.

They even had a soft spot in their hearts for Uncle Joe when he purged all those deviants who were mostly Jewish anyhow.

There's a lot to be said for Iranian president Mahmoud Ahmadinejad. Isn't America the real villain? Insulting the Muslim world with our women in teeny-weeny bikinis. Drinking. Arrogance. Jews running everything. Protesting mosques. Exploiting the Middle East, Africa, and indigenous people everywhere. Supporting the devil, Israel. Who can blame them for hating us?

As for 9/11—maybe we really did drive them to it. As Alice Walker, the Pulitzer Prize–winning author of *The Color Purple*, said, "America and Israel are the real terrorists."

Thank the almighty we have a president who is sensitive enough to apologize for us putting McDonald's everywhere.

And don't think having someone in the White House who loves Islam won't get us loved in the Islam world.

That's liberal thinking.

Who Really Beheaded Daniel Pearl?

Remember Daniel Pearl? He was the *Wall Street Journal* reporter who was beheaded by al-Qaeda in Pakistan for being, among other things, American and Jewish.

He had sought out al-Qaeda to interview. After long negotiations, they granted him permission. They parked in front of his hotel in Karachi and welcomed him into their car with a friendly wave, this liberal, well-liked journalist who wanted to report their side of the story.

They drove him to a house squeezed in among many Pakistani houses and kept him prisoner for several weeks until they beheaded him. All this was captured on video, complete with screams—and they distributed it widely in case anyone might think they were softies.

Danny's widow, who gave birth to their son after his death, wrote a book about the nightmare. Angelina Jolie and Brad Pitt made it into a movie. They added one thing that was not in the book—an explanation of why it happened.*

---

* Not mentioned in the movie was the unpublicized visit by Laura Bush and her daughters to Mrs. Pearl while her husband was held captive. Also not mentioned was the support given her by Pakistani President Musharraf, who asked her not to judge all Pakistanis by these monsters. Why, he asked, did he go with them? He was, of course, deposed.

It was poverty and oppression that killed Daniel Pearl, the movie explained. Millions of people living in squalor and exploited by the West could hardly be blamed for their rage. We arrogant Americans were just as guilty as if we had gripped his head with our own hands and drawn the knife across his neck as his screams pierced the walls of the homes around him. It is America that has committed crimes against much of the world. It is America that has driven them to fight back in any way possible.

Who can blame them?

Ask any liberal.

"Before you shoot that woman taking a grenade out of her burka, you'd better know how to write a detailed report."
—Chris Kyle, the sharpshooter with the most kills in American military history

Until compassionate liberals stepped in to expose the crimes of the military, our bloodthirsty, trigger-happy, sadistic American troops could get away with killing the enemy. Now we're killing our troops with paperwork.

If you read *American Sniper* by former Navy SEAL Chris Kyle, you'll see how successful they've been. Every time he made a kill, he writes that he had to fill out an Assessment Sheet providing the name of a witness to his action, plus the time, place, distance, what he was doing, where he was standing, and what he was wearing. Would the politicians put him on trial?

That's no way to win a war, he says, this Texan who scored 260 kills and is proud of it. Well, Chris, any liberal will tell you that winning isn't everything, not if you have to sink to your enemy's level. Our CIA guys found that out when Obama came in and put them on trial for abusing terrorists with waterboarding. Not to mention sending them to foreign jails for enhanced interrogation. Maybe it got us some information, but we're better than that.

After all, our enemies are people too, with wives, children, and parents, which is why one of the great liberal wins was having journalists embedded with our troops. That keeps them civilized in spite of killers like Kyle who said, without an ounce of compassion, "I didn't go to Iraq to serve our enemies tea and cookies."

He clearly is in need of some sensitivity training.

He adds, after discovering heads and other bloody body parts in several abandoned houses, "The Iraqis are a despicable people."

And Bush gave that guy a medal! No wonder they board planes with bombs in their underwear.

Meet Buff, Pussy, Joy, and Zip
Know Your Teachers Meeting
Friday, 8:00 p.m.

We are happy to announce the addition to our faculty of four professional pornography performers to teach our newly mandated classes: Sex 1 and 2. Thanks to a federal program with generous funding, our children will learn to be comfortable with the naked body—their own and everyone else's. They will acquire the skills needed to maximize gratification at all levels of development, so critical in our society where texting is preferred over actually talking to someone in person.

The classes will go beyond lectures with slides and pointers to include actual interactive experiences in which everyone participates. Our children will learn that there is no right or wrong way to experience sex; there are a variety of ways to enjoy it, each as acceptable and joyous as the other, whether it is male-female, female-female, or male-male—as well as threesomes and foursomes. And, of course, a healthy mix of race and age.

There have been objections, of course, from the usual right-wing spoilers, but those people have been dealt with and we can now bring sex education to its most effective level, beginning with kindergarten.

Let's put our hands together for these new teachers who will bring their lesson plans to life in the auditorium on Friday night. Come and get involved. No cameras or cell phones please.

You'll have no place to put them anyhow.

Furs Come Out of the Closet

Those furs hidden in the back of the closet are coming out. The PETA people are tossing away the spray paint—in the appropriate recycling container, of course—and are remodeling their foxes. So, go ahead and give that ugly down-filled Mao coat to the cleaning lady. Or man.

Furs are coming out everywhere. Gorgeous new styles. Daytime furs. Evening furs. Workout furs. Furs for men. Furs for women. Furs for toddlers. Furs for pets.

Those animals we worried about going extinct have been reclassified. They went from *endangered* creatures that *need to be saved* to *snarling, biting, ungrateful pests that deserve to be offed.* They can contribute far more to the planet by giving up their skins than by gobbling up smaller animals, defecating all over the place, and biting the hands that feed them. They eat our chickens.

So fling open the closet door and bring out that dead mink. Better yet, get a new one. Get a variety. Get jackets. Stoles. Vests. Hats. Sable. Lynx. Chinchilla. You'll feel better for it and you'll look great at the next silent auction to fight climate change.

The More Guns, the Safer
What Happened in Kennesaw, Georgia, and Morton Grove, Illinois
1982

In 1982, the progressive city of Morton Grove, Illinois, banned guns for everyone but police officers. At about the same time, the city of Kennesaw, Georgia, in redneck country, passed a law requiring the head of every household to own a gun.

Both cities were about the same size, and both were middle class. But in one every home had a gun. In the other you wouldn't find a gun anywhere. The result? Liberals have never gotten over this, but the murder rate went up in Morton Grove and down in Kennesaw. Yes, *up* where there were no guns, *down* where everyone was armed—in fact, down to zero for the next twenty-five years when the experts were keeping track of both cities. This proves, believe it or not, that if you want to stop crime, supply everyone with a gun.

That isn't the conclusion that liberals wanted. When they make up their minds, they don't want to be confused with facts. But the fact is that four thousand times a day guns protect people from crime. Guns are fifty times more likely to prevent crime than to cause it.[*]

Of course, liberals aren't going to believe facts they don't like. They want real gun control where only the government is armed.

Their government.

In Florida, a released mental patient went into a gun store and bought a gun and killed someone. The gun store owner had checked on the man as the law required, but was not told the man's mental condition because of privacy laws. When everyone is protected, no one is safe.

---

[*] "Huckabee," Fox News, December 12, 2012.

Don't let those right-wingers make you the fall girl, Hillary.

As for that incident at our Libyan embassy, in which terrorists murdered our ambassador and three other Americans, don't take the blame for not providing sufficient security. Put the blame where it belongs. You know what I mean:

If Bush hadn't attacked the Taliban in Afghanistan and dispatched Saddam Hussein in Iraq—get the idea? *Bush did it.*

The Mamlouks Are Here

Who?

The Mamlouks.

Who the hell are the Mamlouks?

Very few people outside of Egypt have heard of these buggers. It isn't the kind of thing you want to get around if you're a sensitive Egyptian who wants to gloss over a few embarrassments in your history.

The Mamlouks were brought to Egypt from the Caucasus as slaves in the ninth century and ended up running the country. Fit, fearless, and smart, they served as slave-soldiers at first, moved into government positions, and eventually became sultans. They ruled their former masters who were too busy debating the important issues like the environment, sexual equality, crocodile rights, and which gods to worship. The natives also did a lot of cavorting, especially when the Mamlouk sultans legalized sniffing ground poppy seeds.

The Mamlouks—big, strapping, cunning people— knew how to manipulate the once proud Egyptians. They played upon the guilty feelings of those sensitive Egyptians who could not atone enough for slavery. They kept the masses content with free bread, camel subsidies, and unlimited clothing-optional parties, which left them too flat out to care about who was running things. Now it was the Mamlouks who were discriminating against the free Egyptians, excluding them from all the important positions of power.

It was somewhat unfair to those Egyptians who had warned against the Mamlouks, but they were overruled by the courts and liberal *newspapyrus* publishers who condemned them for being reactionaries.

Even the sensitive people who had been eager to elevate the Mamlouks began to have second thoughts. They gradually realized they had become second-class citizens in their own country.

But that is ancient history.

Or is it?